ARGENTINA
the people

Greg Nickles

A Bobbie Kalman Book

The Lands, Peoples, and Cultures Series

 Crabtree Publishing Company

www.crabtreebooks.com

The Lands, Peoples, and Cultures Series

Created by Bobbie Kalman

Coordinating editor
Ellen Rodger

Project development, photoresearch, and design
First Folio Resource Group, Inc.
Erinn Banting
Pauline Beggs
Tom Dart
Kathryn Lane
Alana Perez
Debbie Smith

Editing
Jessica Rudolph

Separations and film
Embassy Graphics

Printer
Worzalla Publishing Company

Consultants
Pampa Risso Patrón, Pan American Cultural Exchange, Houston, Texas; Roberto Risso Patrón; Diana Pelenur, Consulate General of the Republic of Argentina in Montreal

Photographs
AP Photo: p. 11 (bottom), p. 13 (top), p. 27 (left, top right); Archive Photos: p. 9 (bottom), p. 12 (top); Bristol City Museum and Art Gallery, UK/Bridgeman Art Library: p. 8 (top); Corbis/Bettman: p. 11 (top), p. 27 (bottom right); Corbis/Pablo Corral: title page, p. 14, p. 19 (left), p. 25 (bottom); Corbis/Miki Dratsman: p. 24 (right); Corbis/Owen Franken: p. 15 (right), p. 19 (top right), p. 24 (left);

Corbis/Kit Houghton Photography: cover; Corbis/Hulton-Deutsch Collection: p. 10 (top), p. 22; Corbis/The Mariners' Museum: p. 10 (bottom); Corbis/Caroline Penn: p. 5 (top), p. 17 (both); Corbis/Vittoriano Rastelli: p. 25 (top); Corbis/Galen Rowell: p. 15 (top left); Corbis/Hubert Stadler: p. 6 (bottom), p. 20; Corbis/Robert van der Hilst: p. 3; Mary Evans Picture Library/Photo Researchers: p. 8 (bottom); David R. Frazier/Photo Researchers: p. 31 (right); Aldo Frongia/LZ Producciones: p. 29; Beryl Goldberg: p. 31 (left); Julio Pantoja/Infoto: p. 4 (bottom), p. 6 (top), p. 7 (both), p. 15 (bottom left), p. 23 (top), p. 30; Adrian Perèz/Infoto: p. 12 (bottom); Christopher Pillitz/Impact: p. 16 (top); Private Collection/Bridgeman Art Library: p. 9 (top); Chris R. Sharp/DDB Stock Photo: p. 21 (right), p. 23 (bottom), p. 26 (left); Nesor Troncoso/LZ Producciones: p. 16 (bottom); Leonardo Zavattaro/LZ Producciones: p. 4 (top), p. 5 (bottom), p. 13 (bottom), p. 19 (bottom right), p. 18, p. 21 (left), p. 26 (right), p. 28 (both)

Illustrations
Dianne Eastman: icon
David Wysotski, Allure Illustrations: back cover

Cover: Two *gauchos* herd their cattle on the Pampa plains, in central Argentina.

Title page: A group of children play outside their apartment building in Buenos Aires.

Icon: A special cup and *bombilla* straw are used by Argentines to drink *mate*.

Back cover: The nine-banded armadillo is protected by an armor made up of nine individual plates, or sections.

Published by
Crabtree Publishing Company

PMB 16A
350 Fifth Avenue
Suite 3308
New York
N.Y. 10118

612 Welland Avenue
St. Catharines
Ontario, Canada
L2M 5V6

73 Lime Walk
Headington
Oxford OX3 7AD
United Kingdom

Cataloging in Publication Data
Nickles, Greg, 1969-
    Argentina: the people/Greg Nickles.
    p.cm. -- (The lands, peoples, and cultures series)
Includes index.
    ISBN 0-86505-245-X (RLB) -- ISBN 0-86505-325-1 (pbk.)
    1. Argentina--Social life and customs--Juvenile literature. 2. Argentina--History--Juvenile literature. [1. Argentina.]
I. Title. II. Series.
F2810 .N54 2000
982--dc21

00-043222
LC

Contents

Argentina's streets and workplaces are filled with the faces of people from many different backgrounds. Some are the **descendants** of **immigrants** who arrived from other countries during the last few centuries. Others are related to Native peoples who have lived on the land for thousands of years. All celebrate their own customs and traditions.

A troubled history

Throughout their history, Argentines have lived through many difficult times. From the time their country was formed in the 1800s through most of the twentieth century, they have suffered under military rulers and wars. Today, Argentines are proud to have a **democratic** government and are working together to rebuild their country.

This young woman's straw hat and scarf protect her from the hot sun in Formosa, in northeast Argentina.

At the end of recess, these young boys line up to go back to class.

A ranch owner takes a stroll on his estancia *in Patagonia.*

A family takes part in a bicycle marathon in Buenos Aires.

First peoples

Long before the country of Argentina existed, its land was inhabited by Native peoples. Their **ancestors** came to this region in search of food and new lands about 12,000 years ago. By the time explorers from Spain visited in the 1500s, there were about 100 different Native groups in the area, each with its own culture, language, and traditions.

Before the Europeans

Before the arrival of European explorers and settlers, Native peoples in the northwest lived in villages, in buildings made of stone. Their settlements were surrounded by farmland. Native peoples in the northeast lived along the banks of rivers where they fished. To the south were small settlements where people hunted and farmed. Throughout these regions, groups of **nomads** constantly traveled in search of animals and plants to eat.

This mummy of a member of the Diaguita people was found in northwest Argentina. It is between 1,500 and 2,000 years old.

Hundreds of hands decorate the walls of the caves in Los Manos, Patagonia.

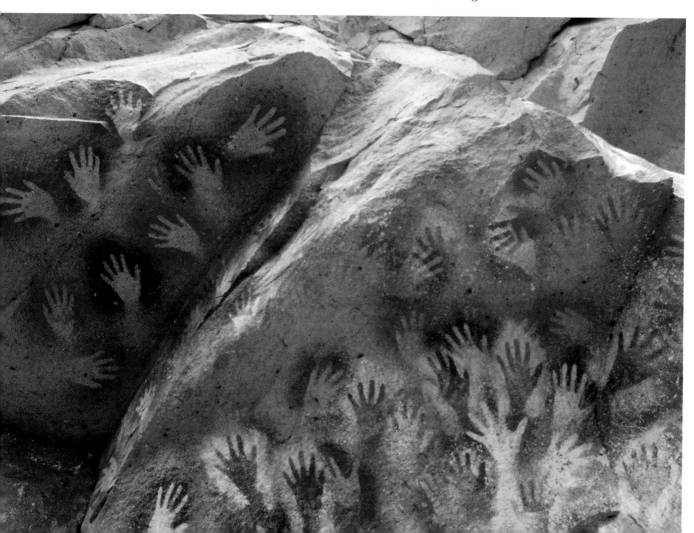

Bones, tools, and art

Archeologists have unearthed Native **artifacts** throughout the country. These include pottery, copper and bronze metalwork, and wood carvings. The oldest artifacts are ancient bone and stone tools, left by hunters about 9,000 years ago in southern caves. At sites such as the Cave of the Painted Hands, unknown artists decorated the walls with paintings of their hands. Paintings of footprints, hunting scenes, and geometric patterns have also been found.

Standing stones

Native peoples built menhirs, or tall stones, that stand in a northern valley called Tafí del Valle. They were probably created about 2,000 years ago. Patterns, including human faces, are carved into the menhirs, some of which are ten feet (three meters) high.

Traces of the Inca

In the far northwest mountains of the country are the ruins of the Inca people. Their huge kingdom ruled the area until Spanish soldiers defeated them in the early 1500s. Highly skilled Inca **masons** did expert stonework. They built fine forts called *pucaras* and a great road called the Route of the Incas.

A tall menhir with two faces carved into it stands in the Tafí del Valle in Tucumán, in northern Argentina.

The ruins at Pucará de Tilcara in northwest Argentina are all that remain of a village inhabited by the Omagüaca people over 1,000 years ago.

Struggle and success

The people of Argentina have a long history of struggle, but they have also had great successes. Many brave men and women helped build Argentina, battled in its wars, and fought against corrupt rulers.

Daring explorers

In the early 1500s, before there was a country of Argentina, explorers came from Spain, searching for silver, gold, and other treasures. Sailing to unknown places in small ships was very dangerous. The first Spanish explorer to visit the area, Juan Díaz de Solís, died in a fight with Native peoples soon after he landed in 1516. In 1520, Ferdinand Magellan stopped on the tip of South America while on a trip around the world. Magellan died on the voyage. Sebastian Cabot came in 1526, naming the Río de la Plata or "Silver River" in the hope it would lead him to many riches. Cabot found no wealth, but at least he returned home safely!

(left) Sebastian Cabot spent three years exploring Argentina before returning to Spain.

(below) In this drawing, Magellan and his crew round Cape Horn, at the southern tip of Tierra del Fuego.

This engraving shows a battle in 1535 between the Querandí people and the Spanish settlers at Buenos Aires.

A Spanish colony

Even though the Spanish explorers did not find any riches, they claimed the land for their king. Over the next 300 years, Argentina, along with most of South America, was a **colony** of Spain. Thousands of Spanish settlers came to build homes, forts, mines, and ports. They established Buenos Aires, which is now Argentina's **capital,** and set up large farms, called *estancias.*

The Spanish settlers changed forever the lives of the Native peoples who lived there before them. They took away the Native people's land and forced many to work as slaves or to fight in their wars. Thousands of Native people were killed. Many more died from diseases the settlers unknowingly carried from Europe.

Fighting for independence

In 1806 and 1807, the British invaded the land. They were forced out by the local people and the Spanish rulers. By this time, many settlers were also unhappy with Spanish rule. They complained that Spain took away their hard-earned wealth and much of their freedom. On May 25, 1810, the settlers rose up against the Spanish rulers and organized the first local government. They fought for six years before they finally won independence from Spain, on July 9, 1816. They named their new country the United Provinces of the Río de la Plata.

General José de San Martín

One of Argentina's greatest heroes is General José de San Martín, a brilliant leader in the 1816 war for independence. With the help of **revolutionary** leader Simón Bolívar, he also helped two neighboring countries gain independence from Spain: Chile in 1817 and Peru in 1821. Today, nearly every Argentine town and city has a statue and street named in his honor.

A fort on the coast of the Río de la Plata protects Buenos Aires from invasion in 1820.

*Workers construct the battleship **Moreno** for the Argentine navy in 1915.*

War and peace

Despite its great victories against the Spanish, there was no peace in the new United Provinces. The leaders of Buenos Aires wanted a central government. The leaders of the provinces wanted independent provincial governments. The different groups battled for their rights. Then, in 1829, Juan Manuel de Rosas, who was governor of Buenos Aires, took over the country and became a **dictator**. Rosas terrorized everyone over the next 20 years, until Justo José de Urguiza defeated Rosas's army.

A united Argentina

Urguiza and the governors of the provinces formed the Confederación Argentina in 1853. This Confederation adopted the first **constitution**, based on that of the United States, and Urguiza was elected the first president.

Over time, Argentina's government developed the country by building public schools and railroads, and by encouraging trade and immigration. It promoted large-scale beef and wheat farming, which made Argentina very wealthy.

Decades of troubles

By the 1920s, Argentina was one of the wealthiest nations in the world. Since that time, however, it has suffered many setbacks. Its elected governments have been overthrown many times by the military, and troubles with the economy have seriously hurt the Argentine people. Both in the 1930s, during a worldwide economic crisis, and after World War II (1939-45), Argentina lost a great deal of income that it earned from **exports**. Many people lost their jobs.

Military rule

As the country's problems grew in the 1930s, the military forced Argentina's elected leaders from power. The military rulers were very harsh. They allowed the people little say in their government's decisions and arrested anyone who opposed them. The military returned control of the country to elected leaders a few years later, but soon overthrew them again. Over the next 50 years, the military repeated this pattern many times, bringing Argentina to near-ruin.

Citizens crowd into the streets of Buenos Aires on September 17, 1930, after the fall of President Irigoyen. Irigoyen was removed from office by Argentina's military.

Juan and Eva Perón

Juan Domingo Perón and his wife Eva Duarte de Perón were two of Argentina's most controversial leaders. Juan Perón was an army colonel when he met and married Eva Duarte, a young Argentine actress.

After Juan was elected president in 1946, he and Eva worked to raise wages, enforce laws against child labor, and improve people's living conditions. Rising to power from a life of poverty in the countryside, Eva became a huge national hero, lovingly called "Evita." She established hundreds of new schools and hospitals, and gave money to the poor. Her death in 1952 from cancer shocked the world. Today, millions of people continue to visit her grave, upon which is written, "Don't cry for me Argentina."

Over time, Juan became a dictator, arresting and torturing anyone who opposed him. He was overthrown in 1955 but was re-elected in 1973, serving until his death in 1974.

Che Guevara

Ernesto Guevara, nicknamed "Che," is one of the most famous Argentines in the world. A doctor by training, he became a hero of the revolution on the Caribbean island of Cuba during the 1950s. Guevara remained a revolutionary until he was killed in 1967 while leading rebels against the government in Bolivia, one of Argentina's neighboring countries.

The Mothers of Plaza de Mayo hold up a banner which is covered in pictures of **los Desaparecidos** *or "the Disappeared."*

The Dirty War

In 1976, the military took over Argentina's government again. The country's new rulers were some of the cruelest it had ever seen. During their years in power, they captured, tortured, and murdered thousands of Argentines who opposed them. This attack on the people became known throughout the country as The Dirty War. The people killed by the government are remembered as *los Desaparecidos,* or "the Disappeared," because they were kidnapped secretly, often during the night, and never seen again. No one knows the exact number of *Desaparecidos.* Estimates range from 9,000 to 40,000 people.

Mothers of Plaza de Mayo

Every Thursday afternoon, since Thursday, April 20, 1977, protest marches have been held outside the government buildings at Plaza de Mayo, the main public square in Buenos Aires. Women, known as the Mothers of Plaza de Mayo, and their supporters gather to demand what happened to their sons and daughters during The Dirty War. The mothers wear a white scarf on their head and pin a photo of their missing child to their chest, or carry signs with slogans and pictures. They remind people everywhere of the military rulers' terrible crimes against *los Desaparecidos.*

Over 10,000 people gather in front of the Casa Rosada on December 16, 1982 to protest Argentina's military regime.

War with Great Britain

In 1982, Argentina's military government invaded the tiny Falkland Islands, or Islas Malvinas, which lie off the country's southeast coast. Argentina always claimed these islands as its own because they are connected to the mainland by a **continental shelf**. However, Great Britain gained control of them in 1833 and forced out the Argentine people.

In response to the 1982 attack, the British went to war with Argentina, winning the islands back in 72 days. About 2,000 Argentines and British were wounded or killed. Argentina's military leaders were disgraced by this pointless war. Angry Argentines pressured them to step aside and call elections.

A new hope

Argentina's elected government was returned to power in 1983. Investigations into *los Desaparecidos* began and several military leaders were tried in court and jailed. Slowly, people started to feel safe in their country again.

Today, Argentina's government is working to improve Argentina's economy and solve the problem of poverty. Although there is still much to do, Argentines have new hope for their country's future.

Traders buy and sell stocks in the busy Buenos Aires stock exchange.

A mix of many peoples

Argentina is one of the largest countries in the world. Of the 37 million people who live there, most are descendants of people from Spain and Italy. Many other Europeans also settled in the country, including some from Britain, France, Russia, Germany, Austria, Switzerland, and Poland. Today, only about fifteen percent of Argentines are not descended from Europeans. They include Native peoples as well as recent immigrants from other South American countries, the Middle East, and Asia.

Friends relax on a monument in the Plaza San Martín in Buenos Aires.

Spanish descendants

Hundreds of thousands of immigrants arrived in Argentina from Spain between the 1500s and the mid-1900s. They built schools, industries, and churches that still thrive today. Their culture and language has had the greatest influence on Argentina's people.

In the last 30 years, people of Spanish **heritage** from other South American countries, such as Paraguay, Chile, and Bolivia, have immigrated to Argentina. Most left their **homelands** because of poverty or because their lives were threatened by their government.

Coming from Italy

Italians searching for a better life than in their homeland made up the majority of Argentina's immigrants during the last two centuries. They have influenced the country's arts, food, family traditions, and even language. Today, Argentine Spanish is filled with Italian words, accents, and pronunciations.

From all over Europe

The influences of other European peoples can be seen in Argentina's sports, street names, foods, and festivals. Favorite games such as soccer, tennis, and polo were introduced by the British. French styles of art and architecture can be seen in city museums, galleries, and the buildings that line downtown streets. In Buenos Aires, newspapers and magazines from Europe are sold at newsstands, and in some neighborhoods it is not unusual to hear people speaking English, French, or German.

(left) This young man lives in San Carlos de Bariloche, in Patagonia.

(above) This man is a descendent of Europeans who settled in Argentina over several centuries.

(left) Sitting on his mother's shoulders gives a little boy the perfect view of a parade during the Carnaval celebrations in Tucáman, in northwest Argentina.

15

A group of young men play beautiful music on pan flutes in the Andes region of Argentina.

Native Argentines

Today, very few Native peoples live in Argentina. Disease, slavery, and the Spanish settlers' wars left behind only those who lived in the far north, west, and south. Farming is difficult in these isolated areas and the Native Argentines who still live there suffer from poverty. Often, they raise just enough food to survive and make a little money selling crafts to tourists.

A mixing of traditions

Each of the surviving Native peoples, who include the Coya, Toba, Mapuche, Matacos, Chiriguanos, and Guaraní, has a unique history, language, and set of traditions. Some have mixed their ancestors' traditions with those of the Spanish conquerors. For example, the Diaguita in the far northwest practice both their traditional religion and Christianity, the religion brought from Spain that follows the teachings of Jesus Christ.

Some Native peoples are in danger of dying out. Hardly any members of the Tehuelche people survive on their lands in Argentina's far south. It is already too late for the Ona who lived on the Argentine island of Tierra del Fuego. The last member of this people died in 1987.

A woman carrying her baby on her back sells blankets to passengers on a train near Salta.

From Wales to Argentina

Among the thousands of immigrants who came from Britain to Argentina in the 1800s was a small group of people from Wales. They feared that the English who ruled their homeland were trying to put an end to the Welsh language and traditions. They settled in Argentina in the hope of preserving their culture.

Survival and friendship

In the winter of 1865, a ship carrying the first 184 Welsh settlers landed in Argentina, on the harsh southern coast. Many of these people were miners who knew little about the farming or hunting they would have to do in their new land. Soon, they became desperate for food. Fortunately, members of the local Tehuelche people offered to teach the Welsh to hunt in order to survive. The two peoples soon developed a strong friendship.

Today, the descendants of the Welsh live in many small communities across southern Argentina. They speak Spanish and have adopted the Argentine way of life, but on special occasions they still celebrate the language, music, dance, and poetry of their homeland.

In the Welsh village of Gaiman, a teacher checks her students' homework.

Few African-Argentines

Between the 1500s and 1800s, the Spanish rulers of Argentina allowed people to own and trade slaves from Africa. During these years, Africans helped build Argentina through farming and mining. They lived under terrible conditions, however. Thousands of slaves were promised freedom if they joined the army. As a result, many marched to war, usually in front of the other troops, and most were killed. This situation continued even after slavery was abolished in 1813. Today, very few African-Argentines remain.

Two brothers go for a morning stroll.

Enjoying family and friends

Four generations of a family pose for a picture at a picnic in Salta.

Family and friends are very important in Argentina. Traditionally, Argentine children, parents, grandparents, and even aunts and uncles lived in the same home. Today, it is becoming more common for children and parents to live apart from other family members, especially in cities. Married children, however, may still live with their families because it is difficult to find or afford a new home.

Getting together

The kitchen is a family's favorite meeting place. On most evenings, parents and children gather around the table to enjoy a long meal and conversation. Once in a while, they eat out at a *parilla,* a restaurant that specializes in grilled meats.

Friends and neighbors are welcome guests in Argentine homes. Their get-togethers usually include a barbecue of beef and chicken. After the meal, everyone sings favorite folksongs, accompanied by the music of a guitar, *bombo* drums, or flute. However, the main activity is talking, especially about politics and sports!

Mate

One of the most important rituals shared by friends and family is drinking a strong-tasting drink called *mate.* It is made from the dried leaves of a bush called the *yerba mate.* Native peoples introduced *mate* to European settlers centuries ago.

Traditional rules must be followed each time *mate* is shared. First, the server puts dried *mate* leaves into a cup, which is usually made from a hollowed **gourd.** Water is heated in a *pava,* or kettle, until it is almost ready to boil. The server skillfully pours the water into the cup to make foam on top. Then, she or he drinks the first cup through a metal *bombilla* straw. The *bombilla* has a strainer at the bottom that keeps the leaves in the gourd and out of the drinker's mouth. After refilling the cup, the server passes it to the person on her or his left, who sips the next serving. The cup is refilled and passed along until everyone has had a drink. It is considered impolite to refuse *mate,* to wipe the *bombilla* before you drink, or to spend too long sipping your serving!

Special occasions

Events such as birthdays and weddings are especially important times for families and friends. Most birthdays are celebrated with a party, as in other parts of the world. However, when an Argentine girl turns fifteen, the age at which she is considered old enough to begin dating, she has a special celebration. She dresses in a fancy gown and dances with her friends and relatives, sometimes to the music of a live band.

A man sips mate *through a silver* bombilla.

A grandmother looks at the toy bicycle that her grandson received for his birthday.

At her fifteenth birthday party, a young girl admires her beautiful cake, decorated with roses and ribbons.

 # In the countryside

In many ways, life in Argentina's countryside is the same as it was a hundred years ago. Most people farm for a living, and everyone in the family helps with chores, which include tending crops and raising **livestock.** There are few cars in the countryside, so people get around on foot, bicycle, or horseback. In town, vendors drive horse-drawn carts along unpaved roads, stopping at little shops and houses to sell their goods. People taking their traditional three-hour lunch break can be seen after noon, relaxing in the shady village square.

A fading way of life

Many rural people are proud of their way of life, but poverty and hardship are common. There are few modern conveniences in many parts of the countryside. Hospitals or schools may be far away and offer fewer services than in the city. For many decades, people have moved from the countryside to nearby cities in search of better-paying jobs and a more comfortable life. Others have moved because farm machines are now doing their work and they have no way to make a living. Today, only about one in ten people lives in the countryside.

(top) A roadside shop near Salta sells drinks and snacks to weary travelers.

Farm country

Families who work on Argentina's small farms grow crops to sell at local markets or sometimes simply to feed themselves. Other farmers live and work on very large *estancias,* which are owned by a few wealthy landowners. These farms are in the central and southern parts of the country where the most **fertile** land is found. While people on small farms **cultivate** their land mostly by hand or with the help of horses or oxen, workers on *estancias* use modern machinery. Their work is still very difficult, because the hours are long and the pay is very low.

Homes and mansions

Some country homes are simple. Most are built of adobe, a kind of brick made from sun-dried clay and straw. The simplest homes have straw or mud roofs, and floors made of packed earth. Some do not have electricity or indoor plumbing. Inside, the furniture is very basic and sometimes homemade. Most families on *estancias* live in more comfortable homes provided by their employers. Wealthy landowners live in the *casco de estancia,* which is the main farmhouse. This large, luxurious home has every modern convenience. Many landowners own a second residence, often a luxury apartment, in a nearby city, where they live most of the time and where their children go to school.

A young boy and his father ride a tractor though their field in the Pampa plains.

A child rings the bell at the end of recess at a country school in Formosa. In the countryside, many children have their classes outside, under tents or wooden roofs.

A gaucho's life

For over 300 years, *gauchos* have roamed Argentina's countryside. These legendary cowboys and herdsmen are respected for their rugged lifestyle, horseriding skills, and sense of honor. They are also considered heroes who fought bravely in Argentina's war of independence. Today, calling people *gauchos* in everyday conversation is the same as complimenting their good deeds and loyalty to friends. A person who performs a *gaucho*-like act of generosity is said to have done a *gauchada*.

(top) **Gauchos** *relax, play guitar, and share* **mate** *in this photograph from the early 1900s.*

Legendary *gauchos*

Throughout the 1700s and 1800s, *gauchos* rode the open plains of Argentina. They earned a living by selling the hides and tallow, or fat, of the thousands of wild cattle they rounded up. They spent so much time on horseback that people began to say, "a gaucho without his horse is without his legs."

Gauchos seldom owned much besides their horse, a saddle, a knife, and the clothes on their back, including a wool poncho. They spent months working on the plains, camping outdoors in the heat and cold, eating nothing but beef and drinking *mate.* Often, they slept on the ground under the stars, using their poncho for a blanket and their saddle for a pillow. If they had a family, they would return home to see them once every few months.

*A **china** dresses in a traditional **gaucho** costume for a festival in Salta.*

Las chinas

Traditionally, *gauchos'* wives, known as *chinas*, stayed home while their husbands worked on the plains. *Chinas* were very poor and led very difficult lives. Their homes were simple, with little furniture. They raised their children on their own and lived a lonely life. Their bleak lifestyle has led many people to say that the *chinas* led more heroic lives than the *gauchos*.

Gauchos today

During the last half of the 1800s, millions of new immigrants came to Argentina and settled the open plains where the *gauchos* lived. Most *gauchos* were forced to find new jobs or to move to more remote parts of the country. Today, there are far fewer *gauchos* than in the past. They still spend most days on horseback, but they also do many chores, such as tagging cattle and sheep and mending fences on *estancias*. Sometimes they sleep under the stars, but they also have their own bunkhouses on the *estancias*.

Tools of the trade

Gauchos have many tools that help them with their daily work. These include a sharp, silver knife called a *facón* and a whip to help with herding. *Boleadoras* are their traditional tools, used to capture cattle or hunt wild game. Invented by Native Argentines, *boleadoras* are made of three stones or metal balls wrapped in **rawhide** and held together with strips of leather. When twirled and thrown, a *boleadora* wraps itself around the hind legs of a fleeing animal, tripping it so that it falls to the ground. It takes great skill to twirl the *boleadoras* — it is easy to knock yourself in the head by accident!

*A **gaucho** on horseback herds cattle on an **estancia** on the Pampa plains.*

The vast majority of Argentines live in cities, where tall buildings rise all around. Sidewalks bustle with shoppers, strollers, and people on their way to work. Cars and buses jam the streets. Everyone crowds into local cafés to eat pizza and talk, children play games of soccer in the streets, and families enjoy ice cream in parks.

In the *barrios*

Larger cities such as Buenos Aires, Mendoza, Córdoba, and Rosario have *barrios*, or neighborhoods, where people of the same background live. La Boca, for example, is a famous *barrio* in Buenos Aires where many people of Italian heritage settled. In their *barrio*, new immigrants met others who understood their language and traditions, and enjoyed similar foods and celebrations.

From downtown to the suburbs

Argentine cities are filled with all sorts of homes. The wealthiest families live in luxury downtown apartments or in spacious mansions in old, established *barrios*. Families who live more modestly have two- or three-bedroom apartments in high-rise buildings. Many families also live in the less expensive suburbs, or neighborhoods on the outskirts of town, where there is more space and less traffic. There, they have single-family brick homes much like those in North America, with a yard or garden, and sometimes a swimming pool.

A woman stops on **calle Florida,** *in Buenos Aires, to make a quick phone call.*

Can you count how many dogs this man is walking?

Villas miserias

Not everyone can afford to buy a home or to pay the high prices for rent. Some people can only live on the outskirts of town in tiny houses they build themselves from tin, wood, or whatever other material they can find. These people have created areas, called *villas miserias,* or "misery towns." The *villas miserias* do not have electricity, heat, indoor plumbing, or **sewage** disposal.

At work

Most people who live in the city work in offices, factories, or small businesses. People usually begin their jobs at around eight or nine o'clock in the morning. When they finish depends on whether they take a long lunch, as is traditional, or a short lunch, as is becoming more common in the city. Some people also take a second job to help make ends meet.

People line up outside a theater on the **calle** *Lavalle, in Buenos Aires.*

Late nights on the town

Families in the city eat a late supper, between eight and ten o'clock. Afterward, some people stay home for the rest of the evening, but many others do their shopping, visit a bookstore, or go see a film. City dwellers are known for staying up late. Few people, even children, are in bed before eleven o'clock at night.

A mother and her two children enjoy the shade outside their home in a **villa miseria** *on the outskirts of Buenos Aires.*

A good education is very important to Argentines. Schools, from elementary schools to universities, are free to everyone. There are also private schools that people pay to attend. Children must go to school from the ages of six through sixteen. In the past, many dropped out before then to find a job and help support their family. Today, more and more students finish secondary school.

Getting to school

Throughout Argentina, the school day is broken into two four-hour shifts. Half the students go to school from eight in the morning until noon, while the others go from one o'clock to five in the afternoon. Some students walk, bike, or take a city bus or subway to school. Others ride a *combi.* Parents arrange for this special school bus to pick up and drop off their children every day.

High school students get ready to watch a film in history class.

School days

Once at school, students study history, science, geography, mathematics, art, and foreign languages such as German, Italian, English, and French. Younger students have one short recess break. During this break, they go to the playground to climb, play in sandboxes, skip rope, or kick around a ball. Older students have short breaks between each class.

Since students are at school for only half a day, they eat lunch at home before or after they go to class. Outside of school, some belong to special clubs, sports teams, or music bands.

Dress code

Many students wear uniforms at school. Children in kindergarten wear pink or pastel colors, while elementary and secondary school students can be recognized by their simple *delantales,* or white smocks, which they wear over their everyday clothes. Private school students often wear full uniforms that include a white shirt, tie, jacket, black shoes, and pants for boys and skirts for girls.

A student carefully lights a Bunsen burner for a chemistry experiment.

Great accomplishments

Argentina's schools have educated many people who became known worldwide for their accomplishments. Some have played important roles in politics, while others are known for their work in science, art, and other fields. A few have received Nobel Prizes, special awards that recognize some of the world's greatest achievements.

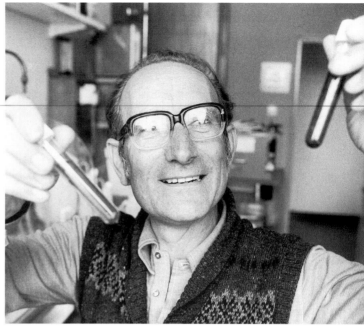

(above) César Milstein (1927-) won the Nobel Prize for Medicine and Physiology in 1980. He pioneered research into the human immune system, which helps fight sickness and disease.

(left) Luis Federico Leloir (1906-1987) was the winner of the Nobel Prize for Chemistry in 1970 for his discoveries about the behavior of sugar molecules.

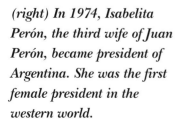

(right) In 1974, Isabelita Perón, the third wife of Juan Perón, became president of Argentina. She was the first female president in the western world.

27

Sports and games

Argentines enjoy many different sports and games. People horseback ride on the plains; ski, hike, and rock climb in the mountains; sail in the oceans and lakes; and play soccer on streets and in parks.

Super soccer

Argentines love basketball, rugby, and cricket, but the sport they love most is soccer. Since it was introduced by British sailors in the 1800s, it has become the country's most popular game. Each week, hundreds of thousands of fans attend soccer games at the many stadiums in Buenos Aires and other large cities. When the national team plays, streets, shops, and restaurants empty as millions of Argentines crowd around their radios and televisions to follow the game.

Soccer players "head," or bounce the soccer ball off their foreheads, in a park in Buenos Aires.

Horseback riding and racing

Throughout Argentina, horseback-riding skills are highly respected. Some people race horses, while others show-jump, leaping fences and other obstacles on their horses. Still others play polo. Two teams, each made up of four riders on horseback, use long mallets to hit a wooden ball across a polo field and through their opponents' goal posts. To keep their ponies from getting injured during the games, the goal posts are made from papier-mâché or light wood. If the ponies run into them while the players are scoring a goal, the goal posts break or collapse. Argentines are some of the world's best polo players, and their strong, fast ponies are in demand all over the world.

Excited soccer fans cheer for their favorite team.

Duck!

Pato is an old and exciting game invented by *gauchos*. Two teams, each with four horseback riders, compete to dunk a leather ball into a net at either end of the *pato* field. The riders must hold the ball, which has six handles, at arm's length so that a passing opponent can grab it away. To keep from losing the ball, riders try to avoid and out-gallop their opponents, or pass the ball to a teammate.

Centuries ago, *pato* was very dangerous. Any number of players could ride on the field at the same time. There were many collisions and riders who fell off their horses were trampled. Players were allowed to lasso opponents or cut free a rider's saddle to keep them from scoring. Most of all, *pato* was unsafe for the duck that was put in a round basket and used as the ball! *Pato,* in fact, is the Spanish word for "duck."

The Clock

With a long jump rope and at least two friends, you can play the simple game called *El Reloj*, or "The Clock," just like Argentine children.

1. Two players hold the ends of a jump rope.

2. They turn the rope as a third player jumps twelve times. While jumping, the player counts from one o'clock to twelve o'clock.

3. To make the game more challenging, jumpers can turn around as they count. They must turn around at "one o'clock" the first time through, at "two o'clock" the second time through, and so on.

Pato *players try to get the ball from one another by grabbing a rope handle.*

Rosa tapped her pencil impatiently on her desk. History class was crawling by. Her mind kept wandering to her cousin María, who was arriving in Buenos Aires this afternoon for a week. María was having trouble with her eyes, so her doctor in the small town where she lived sent her to an eye specialist in the city.

"Rosa," her teacher suddenly called.

Rosa sat up, startled. Everyone was staring at her. "Yes, *Señor* Belgrano?" she asked nervously.

"Will you stop that tapping?" he insisted. "You're distracting the class!"

Rosa was embarrassed. "I'm sorry," she apologized, sitting up and straightening her uniform.

"As I was saying," *Señor* Belgrano continued, "a teacher here became one of *los Desaparecidos* in 1979. The police arrested him after school one day. We were all afraid that we would soon disappear, too."

It was terrible to think that *Señor* Belgrano, such a smart and gentle man, could have been in such danger. Rosa's parents told her many times that she was lucky to have been born after the Dirty War, when people were kidnapped by soldiers and the police.

Rosa was glad when the schoolday ended. As she hurried home through her *barrio,* she thought about her cousin's long bus trip. It had been three years since the cousins last saw each other, and Rosa wondered whether María still liked horseback riding.

A crowded bus rushed by, honking noisily at the cars on the busy street. Rosa turned the corner, passing the Italian bakery, the newsstand, and the café before she came to the entrance of her apartment building.

María watches intently as people play a game of soccer in the park. Rosa is distracted by a group of children nearby.

Rosa and her family live in one of the many big apartment buildings in Buenos Aires.

María arrived almost an hour later. Rosa immediately rushed to give her a hug, then took her cousin's hand. "I have an exciting time planned for us," she said, leading her inside. "Mamá has a special dinner planned tonight, and Papá has promised afterward to play his flute while I play guitar. On the weekend, we'll go to the cinema and the parks, and I'm going to take you window shopping on *calle* Florida, a street that's closed to traffic."

María raised her eyebrows, her forehead wrinkling. "I'm exhausted just thinking of it all!" she exclaimed. "We don't have all of that stuff at home!"

By ten o'clock that evening, dinner was finished and everyone was chatting around the table. Rosa groaned when she heard Papá and her older brother, Martín, talking about soccer again. Couldn't they talk about anything else?

"The salad and steaks were wonderful. Thank you," said María to her aunt.

Rosa's mother smiled and said, "You're welcome." Then, she added, "Is everything all right, María? You seem nervous."

María sighed heavily. "I'm just a little afraid about seeing the specialist tomorrow and I feel so out of place in Buenos Aires. It's so big and there are so many people. I know mostly everyone in my little town. Here, I know only the four of you."

"Well, I think you already know one thing about everyone in Buenos Aires," Mamá said as she rose from the table and walked to the cupboard. She pulled out a special cup and *bombilla*.

María chuckled and smiled. "You all drink *mate*, too!"

Rosa was glad to hear her cousin finally laugh. It was going to be a fun week!

María is surprised to see so many big buildings, cars, and people on the busy streets of Buenos Aires.

31

Glossary

ancestor A person from whom one is descended

artifact A product made by human craft, usually historical

capital A city where the government of a state or country is located

colony An area controlled by a distant country

constitution A set of rules, laws, or customs of a government or any other institution

continental shelf The land beneath the ocean that borders continents

cultivate To prepare and take care of land, by plowing for growing crops

democratic Elected by the people

descendant A person who can trace his or her family roots to a certain family or group

dictator A ruler who has complete power

exports Goods sold to another country

fertile Able to produce abundant crops or vegetation

gourd The hard-shelled fruit of certain vines, which is dried and used to make cups, bowls, and other utensils

heritage Customs, objects, and achievements handed down from earlier generations

homeland An area that is identified with a particular group of people

immigrant A person who settles in another country

livestock Farm animals

mason A person who builds with stone or brick

nomad A person with no fixed home who moves from place to place in search of food and shelter

rawhide The hide of a cattle or other animal that has not been tanned

revolutionary A person who brings about or supports the overthrow or replacement of a government

sewage Waste carried off in sewers or drains

Index

1 2 3 4 5 6 7 8 9 0 Printed in the USA 5 4 3 2 1 0 9 8 7 6